Sports Superstars

Dwyane Wade

Basketball Star

Mary Ann Hoffman

PowerKiDS press.

New York

Published in 2007 by The Rosen Publishing Group, Inc.
29 East 21st Street, New York, NY 10010

Book Design: Daniel Hosek

Photo Credits: Cover © Doug Pensinger/Getty Images; p. 5 © Jeff Gross/Getty Images; p. 7 © Andy Lyons/Getty Images; p. 9 © Stephen Dunn/Getty Images; p. 11 © Jed Jacobsohn/Getty Images; p. 13 © Eliot J. Schechter/Getty Images; p. 15 © Stuart Hannagan/Getty Images; pp. 17, 19, 21 © Ronald Martinez/Getty Images.

Library of Congress Cataloging-in-Publication Data

Hoffman, Mary Ann, 1947-
  Dwyane Wade : basketball star / Mary Ann Hoffman.
      p. cm. - (Sports superstars)
  Includes index.
  ISBN-13: 978-1-4042-3536-1
  ISBN-10: 1-4042-3536-1
  1. Wade, Dwyane, 1982--Juvenile literature. 2. Basketball players-United States-Biography-Juvenile literature. I. Title. II. Series.
 ·GV884.W23H64 2007
 796.323092-dc22
 (B)

37777002766947

2006016104

Manufactured in the United States of America

Contents

Dwyane Wade plays basketball for the Miami Heat. He is an NBA star!

In college, Dwyane led his team to the Final Four. That means his team was one of the best in the country.

7

Dwyane was 21 when he joined the Miami Heat in 2003. He was the youngest player ever to start an opening game for the Heat!

9

In 2004, Dwyane was named one o
the best rookies in the NBA.

11

Dwyane can jump very high and run very fast. He is sometimes called Flash.

13

In 2004, Dwyane was chosen to play for the USA in the Olympics. Team USA came in third.

In 2005 and 2006, Dwyane was named an NBA All-Star.

17

Dwyane scored many points in the All-Star Games.

Dwyane has won awards for his many skills.

PLAYSTATION
SKILLS CHALLENGE

21

Glossary

All-Star (AHL–STAHR) One of the best players in a sport.

college (KAH-lihj) A school you go to after high school.

Final Four (FY-nuhl FOHR) The last four college teams that play to decide which is the best team.

NBA (EN-BEE-AY) The National Basketball Association.

Olympics (uh-LIHM-pihks) A set of games played by sports teams from around the world. The Olympics take place every 4 years.

rookie (RU-kee) Someone who is in their first year in a sport.

Books and Web Sites

BOOKS:

Savage, Jeff. *Dwyane Wade*. Minneapolis, MN: First Avenue Editions, 2006.

Smallwood, John. *Before They Were Stars*. New York: Scholastic, Inc., 2003.

WEB SITES:

Due to the changing nature of Internet links, PowerKids Press has developed an online list of Web sites related to the subject of this book. This site is updated regularly. Please use this link to access the list:

http://www.powerkidslinks.com/spsuper/wade/

Index